UNEARTH

Crab Orchard Series in Poetry
Editor's Selection

UNEARTH

CHAD DAVIDSON

Crab Orchard Review &
Southern Illinois University Press
CARBONDALE

Southern Illinois University Press
www.siupress.com

23 22 21 20   4 3 2 1

Cover illustration: *Planet IX*, by Casey McGuire and
Mark Schoon, from the series *The Great Moon Hoax*

The Crab Orchard Series in Poetry is a joint publishing venture of Southern
Illinois University Press and *Crab Orchard Review*. This series has been
made possible by the generous support of the Office of the President of
Southern Illinois University and the Office of the Vice Chancellor for
Academic Affairs and Provost at Southern Illinois University Carbondale.

Editor of the Crab Orchard Series in Poetry: Jon Tribble

Library of Congress Cataloging-in-Publication Data
Names: Davidson, Chad, 1970– author.
Title: Unearth / Chad Davidson.
Description: Carbondale : Crab Orchard Review & Southern Illinois
   University Press, [2020] | Series: Crab Orchard series in poetry
Identifiers: LCCN 2019023356 (print) | LCCN 2019023357 (ebook)
   | ISBN 9780809337712 (paperback) | ISBN 9780809337729 (ebook)
Classification: LCC PS3604.A946 A6 2020 (print) | LCC PS3604.A946
   (ebook) | DDC 811/.6—dc23
LC record available at https://lccn.loc.gov/2019023356
LC ebook record available at https://lccn.loc.gov/2019023357

CONTENTS

ACKNOWLEDGMENTS

Grateful acknowledgment is made to the editors of the following publications, in which poems from this book originally appeared, though sometimes in slightly different form.

AGNI: "The Minor Castles of Ireland"
Birmingham Poetry Review: "The Brass Disc," "The Field, a Series of Low Buildings, a Distant Road," and "Unearth"
Gettysburg Review: "Disaster Scenes in Language Books"
Green Mountains Review: "Aftermath," "Partially Completed Model of a Sailing Ship," "The Hurt," "United States," and "The Wreck"
Hopkins Review: "A Body in Motion" and "Wake"
Kenyon Review: "Love Poem"
McNeese Review: "Silver Apricot of Japan"
North American Review: "Dumb American" and "How Am I Driving?"
Yale Review: "Roundabout"
32 Poems Magazine: "Ancient Romans"

"Frozen Music" appeared in *The Book of Scented Things: 100 Contemporary Poems about Perfume* (Literary House Press, 2014). "Silver Apricot of Japan" (under the title "Ginkgo") appeared in *Southern Poetry Anthology* (Texas Review Press, 2013).

UNEARTH

I.

UNEARTH

Grainy photos served as introduction
to the hostile atmosphere. All the forms
we had to sign, the rights we waived,

not as we wave goodbye, or are taken
under by the sea. There would be men,
they said, who handle the details:

the packing and ignition, crater
formed from touching down, shortness
of our breath in such surroundings.

To carry all that cargo, all that mess
of past and present failures, to haul
it where we did feels scarcely more

than fiction now. Yet how
unassuming, we thought, the vegetation,
its resemblance to the green we knew

back home, unearthly only in
its sudden presence. It felt unsafe
to stand. We could call the mission

a success, I guess, though surely that's perverse.
We got what we went there for
or, rather, gave it to the dirt,

then filled it back as if to fool ourselves.
I hear the stillness there has amplified,
even with the highway's roar

just outside the gates. Not sure
I could even find it on a map,
let alone in person. *In the flesh*, I'd say,

if not speaking of my mother's grave.

ROUNDABOUT

As Odysseus finds his portal
to the underworld,

delivers his libations, I kill time
just down the shore,

a page or two away, in the blur
the book becomes

after taking off my glasses.
Such trouble seeing,

Tiresias must think, and why
Odysseus goes there.

Once I almost killed some folks is not
a known beginning

to any passage of the *Odyssey*,
though in Anzio,

just south of Rome, I almost did.
Rental car. Mist and night.

I had been drinking is sort of how
the Greek bard starts

his tale, and how I almost ended
everything.

You don't come back from that,
is probably what,

watching Odysseus set out,
Circe thought.

I thought the guy would kill me.
He earned that

dispensation, I suppose, from whatever
held my car

a second in that roundabout.
Not one blemish

on the bright red scooter ferrying them
right up to the edge

of my last night in Italy, and far beyond.
I cannot see beyond that

bright nontragedy, and yet
return again, again

in mist, unlike the hero, man
of many turns,

who beholds his mother's shade
in Erebus,

and three times tries to grasp her,
to earn his passage home.

THE BRASS DISC

in the floor of the Church of Saint Ignatius, Rome

In June's blur and buzz of Vespas I arrive,
the cobbles almost forging faith in me
and my wrecked feet. Inside, the fresco
opens its own sky, the dome faked
with such panache, such trust in the eternal
lie, I swear dust floats in the nets
of late sun in the transept. Just as it was
ten years back, when my mother looked
like any other tourist, head cocked to take in
the barrage. She watched Ignatius in ascent
amid crowds like those we left sweltering
in the piazza. Last time I saw her
amazed. At least in another country.
Because in the hospital, years after, yellowed
from sepsis, she gazed through morphine
fog with the same unearthly eyes.

It's all a joke. From anywhere but the disc
mortared in the floor, Pozzo's dream
of wholeness shifts to two dimensions,
its perspective cocked. Step away,
and you confront this fact: heaven
is stuccoed over. The sky? Apprentice work,
the master busy with that bald saint
hoisted by a gang of cherubs toward the Lord,
who, since held aloft by trickery, frightens
with the massive cross He bears. A tourist,
I linger for my chance, deliberate as bone,
to stand on that baroque skeleton
key of a disc, opening every possible vision.
My mother is here, and not in the way
we dream the dead are somehow *with us*.
She's the sallow Japanese woman

in a soft hat, mouth agape, wrenching her neck.
The German girl who smiles with the openness
of the first telescope aimed at the heavens.
Me and my failure to remember the date
of church construction, the patrons, the meaning
of those animals, all of them present here:
the world at the center of the world.

The trouble with church is gravity:
travertine, the chunky columns, foundations
deep in earth—all in the name
of lightness, spiritus, breath. Paradox
and untruth. Here, at least I'm in control
of my illusion, even willing to give in.
Some arrive to watch the sky come
into focus, the dome reveal its depth.
Some recall the thrill of everything
just going right again, then wrong, so seek
that happening. Not joy precisely. Rather,
the distances between this time and last.
I am here again. I am always here. I am thrown
back, with my mother, waiting for the flash.

DUMB AMERICAN

The phrase most likely targeted my mother
in the bubble of a two-week trip,
both of us descending through cobbled rivers,

toward the buzzing center of Siena. Still,
with all the goings-on—street sweepers
freighting away last night, the frenzied polishing

of such medieval everything—I heard, or thought
I heard, this man say, *Dumb American*,
this archetype studiously *crucial*:

related to the cross, a coming to terms
in the biblical sense, a reckoning.
I turned and, in Italian, told him,

I understood what you said. And I did.
But didn't. How could I—mother
in tow, Virgiling her through foreign land—

know what to make of his anger formed
three million years ago in the Pliocene sea
that drowned this town and cliffs around it?

All I knew was what heat and pressure does
to stone, turning it a deep red-brown so pretty
on the roofs and pavers, *burnt*, like the face

of the man who thought of us as dumb
Americans, who followed us, cozy in rage
I return to often, turning the moment over,

the way my mother held a wooden cross—
so many in the trinket shops where men
like him labored—and called it beautiful.

PUTTING IN

On an island below Italy, after cocktails,
a lemon tree in a pit by the house
we rented for a week. What lives in recess,
what survives, what can, is bitter.
That house of mortarless stone.
Those gangly roadside caper stems
that left green streaks along our car.
Roads thin enough to keep grief out,
at least sequestered in the port, miles
from our sleep. Our landlord died,
we heard from a neighbor come for lemons.
We capitalized. We were good at that.

When my mother died, the family put in
time sifting through debris. We couldn't
clear it. Or didn't want to. Sewing machines
and tools that cut. Baby shoes, bronzed,
strangely sharp. Dangerously so. Swatches,
frayed remnants of quilting squares, photos
of the year trucks arrived to dig our pool.
Putting in, the workers called it,
though most of it they hauled away.
It took whole crews to carve it out.

WAKE

Casamicciola Terme, Ischia

Look past the ships at port, past Mary,
just a perch for gulls in the harbor's heart.
Look past the ribs of sailboats docked,
locked up till August. Past the sun itself,
which idles like a trawler always almost
ready to reveal its haul. Look past it all,
the bars on wobbly pilings, portly bathers
slick with oil, the Mondrian of beach chairs
lined and stacked or laid out flat. The man
raking grooves in the sand. Look past,
but then: what, then? Just a blue that gathers
at its seams the wakes of hydrofoils, erasing
even them. Heresies come in all the azures,
lapis lazuli, and midnights we can think of.
This one here is nothing special, other than.
Nothing—meaning something far beyond
some matter of chemical alliances, fish
and salt. Besides, the haze is clearing.
Atop the flanks of Vesuvius now, its jagged
rim discernible but just, another opportunity
blown. We are made of such intense regrets.
No taking that back, that or the trawler's catch.
Look at them now unloading all the spoils, curious
word we use for both the bounty and the waste.

PLUTO

We saw photos on the news, almost lunar
in their stark relief, as if demanding
caution, scrutiny, even the anchor
caught in reverence. *Wow*, he said.
You checked the temp of the roast, returned
with tumblers full of some concoction.
I was unimpressed, unlike the planet's skin:
scarred, ridged with craters like the moon.

I puzzled over what the hell it was
about me made me doubt those photos.
Was I seeing what I should not see?
The rain, too: hardly, somehow always
on the verge, our tomatoes split
from ghostly storms we never even woke to,
or from. You fussed with foil and baster
at the oven's mouth, sweating in its breath.

Then the moons appeared, their names
annunciated: Charon, Hydra, Styx—
names as infernal as that August, as maples
acquiesced, kudzu withered, and cocktails
bled on the nebulae of our coffee-table grain.
How could anything survive in that
deep cold? I asked myself, swirling
the ice in my drink with a finger.

COMET

I'd love a revelation, something
for the ages: a comet or just Jesus
for an encore. Instead the trash truck
punishes a dumpster up the street,
and the mail, dressed in white again,
finds me here, at least my name,
at the start of another century.

Sometimes I look at my life
as if it were the Earth
seen from the moon, a flag
stuck there. Other times,
I'm the Earth just spinning
in a cloud of noxious luxury.

Truth is, when you go under,
and the doctors have you count,
you never reach the end. Truth is,
that vestigial tail of the comet
is just the comet burning up.

FIRSTS

First time you prepared us
thyme-and-lemon chicken,
time the vet called while you did.

First time I had to leave
in the middle of your prepping
skin, tightening the truss.

First time I rushed to the vet,
to our first cat, named Starsky,
just like on TV. First time

I paused the world with a click—
a downed Russian plane
and other matters of the heart

frozen on public broadcast.
What did it matter, anyway,
first time I left in sweats,

in sweat—in cold, in rain—
for the vet? You couldn't do it,
couldn't bring yourself to go

or bear to eat alone. You waited,
first time ever, for my return
with whatever passed

for news. First time my arrival came
just after a departure, time
they led me to the inner chambers

of their offices, a shepherd
whining in his kennel. No hope
then for the Russians. No matter

great enough to matter,
as I held Starsky like a parcel
after they had wrapped him

for his journey. *Swaddled*,
I might say, if not for masking tape
that kept the whole thing neat

and clean and bound forever.
First time I used a word like *swaddled*.
First time I had to. Time

I came bearing such a present
for you, present in itself
yet strangely weightless.

Such wreckage in the kitchen,
bones and all, charred fuselage
still floating on the TV screen,

as we went out with a flashlight
and a shovel. One tool for shedding light.
The other for the dirt.

BULLET CREMATION JEWELRY

designed to hold a small portion of ashes, hair, or dried ceremonial flowers
—perfectmemorials.com

Maybe shamrocks for those less-than-pure
Irish, who mostly seek eternity in peat.
The stately fleur-de-lis might signify
your loved one's origins, or just a favorite
running back. Such engravings to consider,
ways to package death as a velocity, sleek yet still

commemorative. Twin stags, a Harley, lightning bolts:
just some of the insignias whereby your lover,
father, mother, dog, or cat will be forever
almost ammunition. The phrase *shot out of a cannon*
seems not so off the mark, as we raise
our polished rifles, fire into heaven

rather than flesh, which always proves
less given to gray elegies the clouds preserve,
accumulate in cumulus. And why not Jet Ski
right across the Lethe? They've designed one
just for that, if design ever govern in a thing
this queer, surely what your neighbor thinks

when you pulverize your horse and pack it
in a shotgun shell. Funny how the dead remain
insistent on potential, ever ready for a coup.
They are, it's true, both immaterial yet all
materiel, the highest caliber and buckshot.
This is why our coffins also look like bullets.

MY DEAD FRIENDS

Some of my best friends, in fact.
A buddy from Texas. Two chums
in California haze, that haze being
such common imagery in passages
to afterlife. Being and not being.
Even pets of friends, buried deep
in the sad stories they repeat, in graves
in backyards all across this nation.
My own cat, for goodness' sake,
just a rock by a tree. Enough
with the notices and obits,
Halloween getups and haunts.
Say *uncle*, and I think of mine,
now dead, who helped me sand my car
to metal for the prime. So many ways
we have to scrub a thing to shine, really
shine, like my mother still does
in photos on her Facebook page.
We're friends, besties, thick as thieves.

Why should I steal some gray, anyway,
from the clouds' silk ribbons unfurling
down this sky today? Why misread the runes
of my mother's posts on social media,
still there for all to see, such prophecy
in pumpkin pie, now five years past,
which she declared a disaster to all
us living souls with constant access
to this day, to trivia and misadventures
in dessert? Sometimes I hear her voice,
dial it up, in fact, on the landline tethered
to the house my father lives in still.
Tethered is a pleasant way of putting it.
I want to tell him to erase it, scrub it clean,
that it's too painful. Like how my wife,

when she wants a cat of ours to sit with her,
will yowl. *They respond to sounds of pain*, she says.
Amen, I say. Yet when I try, when I call out
in my best worst cat, feigning deepest anguish,
they never come. They see right through me.

II.

LOVE POEM

The pigeons of Rome have withered legs
yet still descend in search of decent
condolences. In this way, our crumbs turn
luminous and graceful, like the charming
little lights strung up in storefronts just for us,
like this sunset, Aperol-orange and wedged
in an alley. Whether we grow into men or women,
age becomes a destination, a city, like Rome.
We have traveled here together.
We say we turn luminous, wise with age,
like polished marble or the frankness
of a sculptured horse in the center of this
charming city. Pigeon, if spelled otherwise,
is a language newly formed, wedged
between two others, which, given time,
creates its own friction, problems of meaning.
By the sculptured horse, I should have said,
I love you. My condolences: literally, *with pains*.
Descent just signifies *a falling from*, as in grace,
but seldom do we note what we're falling toward
or in. We say, *It pains me to say this*, and sometimes
it does. *It* is painfully imprecise, this pronoun,
this impersonal thing, which I am not. Let me be
personal: I say *the pigeons of Rome* but often mean
otherwise, which is what I mean right now.

PARTIALLY COMPLETED MODEL OF A SAILING SHIP

We are all unfinished, attendant on a voyage.
We are less the bright, sought-after stateroom,
more the brine on rigging.

My friend left his wife of twenty years
as a ship might sail from a wartime port.

Away from, yet into.

We are the workshop's disarray, not the mantle.

My friend has washed ashore from shipwreck.
He alone escaped, he thinks.

A model is often just a miniature but not always.

The massive whirlpool and stitch of beasts
that skirt the carta's incognita: those, too, are promises.

I helped my friend heap boxes in a truck.

We are such potentialities, maps drawn from fever,
blood from the rope of a vein.

Some models might take years, especially the small ones.
Those no one pays attention to.
Those built inside a bottle or because of.

Who knows how long my friend will last in such conditions.
Malarial the air around each dinner hour, arctic chill of afternoons.

Disasters also tell us stories.

The trick is knowing which presents more fiction.
Or less.

THE WRECK

in the Keats-Shelley House, Rome

Outside, tourists and pigeons scavenge
history for scraps, desperately
at ease in late-summer sun. Inside,
Shelley's jawbone, at least a piece of it.

Some things should not be parceled.
Take beauty, for example. The girl
who led me here, when she explained
the ceiling was original, was. I loved more

the look not *of* but *on* her face,
the way I often fall for space
around a poem, not what lies inside.
So many surfaces in which to finally see

myself wrecked: this jaw or death
mask behind thin glass, the great windows
of these two souls shut tight to the noise.
Our tour finished, the guide returned

to her book and hair. Both fell over her.
Dusk in narrow streets falls suddenly.
I never liked Keats the way I should.
When I think of Shelley, I think of the girl

my sister joked with as a kid. Not a wreck.
Not a bone. Outside, the fountain
in the form of a boat seems particularly
blunt. On the Spanish Steps,

some girls embark on their evening drinking.
The possibilities, they must think, are
enormous. The quality of light, ideal.
The weather, fabulous, and far from Viareggio.

ON NOT SLEEPING

A moon, bright as myth,
scatters in flotsam. Odysseus turns

to depart, yet stories don't
end. He remembers bodies

brushing in a horse's belly
rich with steel and other forms

of hate. Is this where the moon,
he thinks, finally wrenches free

from the tide, shards
glistening in dark grass,

the ringing plains? We repeat this
tale, repeat this tale, repeat this,

says the water to the sand, old lovers
of subtraction. We know nothing,

says Odysseus, of the weather,
not yet. Boarding his ship,

he brushes the back of a rower
whose name he can't recall.

But I, says the sea to the hull,
I remember yours.

ANCIENT ROMANS

I see them dragging their garments
through the frenzied piazzas and rush
of the now, beholding this Rome
they never knew. Empires are funny

that way, all the statues say to them,
so they find a bench, a corner table,
or dangle feet over the stone lip
of a promenade and wonder how

it all came to pass. That sky, too,
they think—the gem of sun
in marbled blue—that will be theirs.
And the hills, obviously—not just

what was built upon them. Given time,
even the stunned gulls will learn
Latin and a penchant for vice, nest
in the crenellations of some fortress,

dreaming of a fortress all their own.
And these streets so fabulously slicked
in blackest rain will go on pulsing
outward from antiquity. Who's to say,

using them, how far these men could travel?
to the ends of Gaul? beyond Dacia?
to those heathens in the islands of death
who may themselves be sipping wine?

But, hey, what's the rush, they think.
They've learned to take their time
far into time, strap it to the mute hordes,
and thus not worry over transport.

That man, a few say, pointing at me.
He'll do just fine. Kind sir, they call,
would you humor us a moment?
We have so much we want to show you.

SILVER APRICOT OF JAPAN

Far too glorious a name for you, conjuror
of stench enough to frighten

atheists back to the dense
underbrush of faith, your linger cruel

as a joke—not the *ha-ha* but the stab,
taunt of the bully.

Dog crap aflame in a paper bag.

A stink much less of death
and more of dying, of bedsores

festering in little, purple lakes.

You just chattered your branches, that winter
we moved in, saying nothing.

Fits of wind summoned by some silver-haired god
in love with the jet stream and bliss

of not knowing, not smelling, racked you to the wall
February made of the sky.

You took it like a captive, then rained down come
spring your vomitous reek

gathered on the paws of cats, wheels of cars, names
of the dead whose mail kept arriving.

I took it all until I couldn't take it—

hacked you back from power lines, or so I told that part
of me that hates the grip
of loppers, grumble of a chain saw.

Still your shit stones seeded planters with their ick.

The trick, a friend advised, is to find some Japanese mystics
to harvest all that funk

for poultices and memory aids.
Teas, he mused, of furious delicacy. God,

let them come in wide hats by mule.

Let them drone their spells, spread tarps
and shake your limbs, ginkgo, for all their worth.

JUDITHS

Dawn arrived in Bethulia with the chatter
of starlings on the temple walls. Pleasant
even that nuisance, she must have thought.
The old order, the usual plagues.

The general, in gold such office calls for,
gathered sun around him, made Judith,
rendered her—how to put it?—more
womanly, her gold pounded thinner yet.

Still, she had her doubts, as some servants
fetched their supper. There are things
even Judith wouldn't do. Besides, it's nice
to know that someone's lower, lesser than.

All evening, the bloodied sun beat itself
against his tent, dragging its regretful tapestries
through first course, second, wine,
until Judith was the only morsel left.

From Ohio, reports of a man with three girls
in his basement and ten years for them
to think about it. The situation what it was,
he had them do much more than think.

The man pled guilty to *937 charges*—a word
as fitting as the next, a number large enough
to carry import, if counted slowly, carried
far enough. He claimed he's not a freak,

just hooked on porn. The girls could not
agree, predisposed to feel that way,
reporters said. Besides, they did survive,
which simply means *to live above* or *past* or

over, as if just living lay beneath, beyond.
All evening now, TVs chatter of a suicide—
the killer—while in jail. It's not death
that troubles, those women must have thought,

but the fact of such untroubled death.
Pain loves a mirror. When they peer in,
they just see women. Hundreds of them,
maybe thousands of artworks, all by men,

feature Judith, though they're split between
the ones who want her hacking through
and those who simply want it done, want more
symmetry: a head, say, on a gilded platter.

UNITED STATES

It is understood geography:
we are not so independent

of each other. Maps confirm
such spread into the West, past

your birthday, for example,
and far into the year. Rivers,

mountains: once they held us
captive to our own intentions—

school, work, this or that
fantastic trip to other states

of fear that we were growing
closer to each other. (*Each other*

comes up often in our talk,
our articles of incorporation.)

The hours spent on planes
thirsty for turbulence, doldrums

of the terminal: landscapes
we mistook for states of being.

That point in life when the point
that separates your love of me

from my frustration with fusion
cooking (though I love you

for the food I find on this,
the most tiring day our country

has endured): we have reached it.
Our long national nightmare

is over. We have survived
our own immaculate sense

of what we wanted from each other,
which was always next to nothing.

THE HURT

Waking from a troubled sleep, I turned
and asked my wife what time it was.
Who are you? she asked. Your husband,
I said. I eat grapefruit, repair the washer.
You're not my husband, she said. Yes,
I am, I said. If you're my husband,
then who prepares the coffee? I do, I said,
every morning. And the glass bottles:
who sorts them lovingly, like a Cyclops
does his cheeses? Me. And the guy
that changes filters, mends the tiny holes
the photos of friends' children make
on our walls? Yours truly. And the car
and its leaky gaskets, the sprouts coaxed
from nothing but a wet paper towel,
the 401(k) and live bird in the maw of our cat
last Tuesday, so helpless, small, and trembling:
if you're my husband, you take care of that?
I nodded. Yeah, right, she said. Right, I said.
I think you should leave, she said,
before my husband wakes up. He'll hurt you.
I tell her that I couldn't hurt a soul,
that in the dream I had last night,
I went to punch a guy, and the air
around my arms grew viscous, weighty,
just like Vaseline. Oh yeah, she said,
if you're my husband, you wouldn't do that.
My husband couldn't hurt a soul.
You're right, I said. It was a dream:
the house with the broken washer,
perforated walls, all the children
smiling from those glossy frames,
the small, trembling tax shelter,
none of it was real. But it is real, she said,
everything but the hurt. That's marriage,

I said, everything *and* the hurt. Right,
she said. Right, I said. So you *are* my husband,
after all, she said. Yes, I said. Then may I
tell you about my dream? she asked.

INSOFAR

In the evening, in the lazy orange like
a chrysalis of Tang, birches wear their clothing
raw, molt on the lawn. Drinks in hand,
we rummage in it all, play at playing,

while neighbor kids peer from the unreal
yellow parapets of their prefab castle.
It even has a flag. Why is it everyone demands
submission? Yet there's a point in evening,

somewhere south of 7:00, when surrender
to a chair in the yard and you with iced gin
is the only territory worth a noble death.
Next door, someone slays someone else,

or so we figure from the hoots. It must be
a reprisal. The sun is orange enough to lick.
The kaffir leaves, like cheap soap, make me dizzy.
Sweetness is a curse but only if we fail

to study all its contours. The way you test
your gin's astringency: that's one. Juniper,
another. And the sleuthing our two cats enact
under the refuse of the birch trees. Let me

refuse your offering of your life to me.
We said it in those vows, but we were lying,
like we do in grass late summer,
our little fiction, insofar as we make it

up, like a bed or kid who's off to church,
insofar as night is just nostalgia
for the evening. I have let myself become
high-minded, unreal. Sweetness is a function

of the sun, insofar as being far away
lends warmth. Any closer and we'd burn,
insofar as we could for each other. So far,
this evening's ending up divine. Come closer.

FROZEN MUSIC

If that's what architecture is, form
from the inner workings of our ears,
some small stage around which windows
sizzle in rain. If what contains us

barely holds a blur of fingers over keys,
handful of catgut strings and guitarist
raising difficult codas in the gel lights,
which almost float among the ficus.

If, given time, song hardens into girder.
If an auditorium's hum and pleasant dark
were darker yet when merely concretized,
then what to make of the mischievous scent

that club in Perugia gave off twenty years ago,
all soft to the nose but barbed underneath,
a handful of forks under a napkin? Understand:
Italy, with its ardent taste for sweet

astringencies—vinegars that disappear
each year further in their tiny balsa, blood
oranges crying on a cutting board,
all the monks sealed in their humilities,

reaping juniper and sage for some elixir
smoke black and metallic, like one's tongue
on a lamppost after rain—pleasure must pass
through fire, must chafe and blister

and, in doing so, make its cure the joy.
Remember those lovers in the front row,
drinking in each other and the tune
we all had heard a hundred times?

And yet that time was different, if only
for the heavy drapes of it unfurling
round them in their own euphoria.
Different because that song was theirs now:

some small rented room with a boiler plate,
a fridge with a few wrinkled pears
inside, gorgonzola wedge, and, as happens
often in paradise, almonds

rusting in a glass dish atop the stereo,
on which plays that song, that song
that erected itself around them, that carried
an odor like money, on fingers, after it is spent.

THE MINOR CASTLES OF IRELAND

The one, for instance, outside Newcastle West,
through whose iron gates a few spaniels darted,
as you wandered outside, stunned in the snowfall
of a ramshackle Christmas fair. Or the ruins in Cong,

where moss glowed on arches leading to the infinite
interiors, it seemed, of grass and placards,
numbers for which you had no audio guide.
Or take Ross Castle in Killarney: just a mass

of dark behind you in the photo snapped
by another tourist, his offer surely some token
of admittance, a gesture toward access.
In the distance, assorted swans disturbed

the lake ice next to a little fishing boat
placed just so, as if constructed for you
in consolation. You know this nothing
is not special. Winter, and the minor castles

lock their turnstiles, switch off the sconced
fluorescence, unplug their radiant pasts,
while snow—the only visitor—filters through
the oaks and ash in striking solemnity, begging you

to look, then look away, as it reorders itself
along the ramparts. The balance, you think, is finally
barely endurable: that snow on the knife of a branch,
that castle just beyond your plunder. It's there,

but it's not. For you, only the major sites remain—
Bunratty with its mock medieval village; Muckross
and its dour guards and entrance fee that sent you
back to the comfort of your rental car

and plain white biscuits in their tin; even Kylemore,
whose gift shop, you swore, boasted Ireland's best
scone, which is, if not outright hyperbole,
surely no major triumph. Just a minor grace

in those blustery two weeks on the western edge
of Europe, poised between the major and less
than minor—that ubiquitous bit of wall
jutting from pasture, or the meager half-

tower that rose from scaffold by the Texaco
in Gort—all left utterly to the steel of the present,
where the heat toggles off, the guidebooks
somehow always in French, a situation

in which the only constant is that slow return
to little more than rubble heaps bereft
of brochures, names. Most of us, you think,
go that way, while only Kylemores, the precious

Muckrosses of the world, enjoy the warmth
of numbers, the numbness that comes from the well
shod fresh from their coaches, which idle
like sheep in enormous car parks. Those other sites,

though, the minor castles of Ireland, seem caught
between celebrity and forgetfulness—
those dueling impressions—depending on the good
weather and a steady dose of your nostalgia

for old Europe. And whether maintained by a gaggle
of teenagers seeking drink money in summer
or that crusty guy in a crusty sweater
who breaks the news that it's closed, the whole

deal is closed, you can't finally understand.
Even if you entered, you wouldn't understand,
caught in your passage southward for the real
past, the best scone, both resembling this man

too usefully quaint to ignore, yet unfit, finally,
for the index of your guidebook, like the ruins
at Kilmacduagh, like all the minor castles,
whose refusal to let you in becomes

your holiday. Of course, you swear, you'll return.
(You're that vain.) But you'll do so knowing
mostly that you're merely answering a call
from someone you no longer are—that guy

in the photo outside Ross Castle, say,
who knew, while staring at the camera,
at that particular moment, nothing
other than that he badly wanted in.

III.

POWER

I thrived in the epoch of cathedrals,
my wife a handmaid in mosaics of Ravenna.
The oddest job I ever held I held the drills
that surgeons used on papal skulls.

So many torture museums, so little time.
So many babes I held before their mothers
screamed for clemency, carts of lime
spread in piazzas. My vespers chime?

Just a shovel on a stone, nothing more.
Who needs a world of such amazing density?
Even bones will offer that and more.
There are chapels in The Eternal City more

bone than simple agape. I confess: I did it
right, carved the arms off dynasties,
skinned a girl not even seventeen, a bit
of flair, a talent with the knife. Each slit

could open continents of grief,
territories ripe for empire, but I drew more
than maps and blood, turned belief
itself to flourish, texture, grand relief.

DISASTER SCENES IN LANGUAGE BOOKS

Michael and Maria look lovely in their boat
before they capsize. Sofie merely hacks
a ripe tomato, while a man and small car meet
outside her window, down some shady avenue
of the German mind. The machine itself
appears to harbor great regret, the grill
pitched back, toward a past that didn't lead
unerringly to mayhem and a lesson on the preterit,
all of us caught in the eternal present
of my bad Deutsch. Don't blame Melanie, either,
who couldn't have foreseen that bit of ice or grease
(the drawing is unclear) that left her speechless,
crying her blank dialog box on the ground floor
of scenario two, Josef left to stare in disbelief.
Things hardly go better for Rolf, who just wants
Hawaii and tiny umbrellas, sloppy poi,
but beholds instead a jet on the tarmac awash
in flames. Can you say *immolation?* Can the grammar
of that burn arrive in any tense but the imperfect?
Each explosion is a prompt, which is how we learn
to write through our disasters—literally *star-crossed,*
unlucky, like Holger, whose moped dies
in the Turkish quarter, which we discover again
behind a train depot, or deposited in glossaries
at the backs of culture chapters. When was it, anyway,
these exercises laid their trip wires, the Claymores
of tricky prepositions? Suffering, we think:
now that's the new normal, like Hans the irritable
schnauzer and the *Schmerz* on Daniel's shin.
Dread holds in place our wounded words
like a splint, while that surly nurse in the cat-print
scrubs just wants it all to heal, wants us
and our penchant for self-harm to convalesce,
to eat the goddamn Jell-O. Pain, in German,
is reflexive, as is this book, teaching me fracture,

fever, third-degree burn. I may not carry conversation
further than I could a victim from the mouth
of his shattered storefront, but I might recommend
a cold remedy, something folksy, which this book
surely reads as retrograde, faulty, like the carburetor
on Holger's moped, or Sofie's knife, which, as it cuts
deep into that tomato, spills the seeds, which,
from this distance, on my tongue, far from the rash
of Turkish spice, remind me of stars, or periods,
or whatever Germans use when they really mean the end.

A BODY IN MOTION

When the pedal snapped clean under my foot
in the city's clotted alleys, in the heart
of Rome, careening my cheap bike sideways,

almost into the café, into tourists with their thriving
pensions and Campari, I just barely hung on.
In a video, some kid dangles from a crane

for fun, far above an avenue's indifference,
people carrying on like needles in the grooves
of their routines. I'm not sure what's worse:

recklessness or exhibitionism, the fact he did it
or that his friend just tagged along to film.
And so the air churns overhead, knocking trees

senseless, shaking sadness out. The ducks
almost offer themselves again to our spoiled cats
half concealed in azalea at the edges of the known.

And somehow we enjoy all this, the nearly tragic.
Caravaggio, mere days from Rome and a pardon,
instead just up and died in Porto Ercole,

and of mysterious causes. Maybe the mystery
is what we wanted all along. No doubt
his studio was drab. He beat his lovers, likely

ate the stale bread. It's not how fast you fall,
my physics teacher told us (we were young,
barely hanging on to ourselves), it's how fast you stop.

AFTERMATH

Some places are more striking when destroyed,
when struck.

We are formed of such rebellions: cancer
in the suburbs, riot in the cell block.

Some things just seem to shine in aftermath, neon glistening
down the dark length
of the half-shelled

remnant of a Berlin church

whose name escapes me.
Names are often the only things that do.

Names for savagery, I mean,
and territories brought to ruin.

That smolder on the roadside.

We ask our televisions what *really* went on
or off

when the backpack blew,

in which desert those women in scarves now seek asylum—
which is no more
than a tent and dirty children eating rice.

Bags of rice, the size of children, airdropped or thrown
from the ass ends of trucks.

Look: there's a guy in a fedora, sleeves rolled up,
a woman in fictitious burka. They're there
to interview survivors.

Our hearts go out
but only as the yo-yo might.

A boat somewhere right now is sinking.
Relocation is preamble to the mortaring.

We are so many easily impressed
systems of belief.

We could build a bomb shelter out of them.

Not the natives, who still can't live on their atoll.
Not the strontium still ravaging, the divers paying all that dough

to pay respects to sharks and Geiger blips
that traffic there.

But the swimsuit named for those explosions,
the bikini,

with which its makers hoped to cause, in Paris,
such a shock.

And did.

PICTURE PERFECT

Every demon is a sweetness, our rituals
shockingly diverse.

Each highway a pigment we grind
deep into winter.

Everything is
hauled, warehoused,
sold dirt cheap.

Everyone's a neighborhood
watch.

We have no mail anymore,
no need.

Our declarations, independent; our voices,
those of grass.

Listen.
We know more than the living.

We are such slow-burning happiness.

Bike streamers and the garishness
of leisure.

Our dangers relegated
to the wasp nest

above our picture window.
Picture is a ghost of a word,

bedridden on the porch
of clichés. We ride all night

into the predicate of perfect sentences.
We *sentence* some

to hard labor, as if we knew less
restrictive grammars.

We watch the men in white jumpsuits
along the skeleton

the new pool complex makes.
Excuse our progress,

reads the sign. Always this
pardon of ourselves, never

someone else.
Pardon me is an imperative.

We are guilty, yet we still command.
Still, such warmth in our book clubs.

Even the mouth
of a volcano, from far away,

is beautiful.

HYMN

Let us praise the pastor
in any one disaster,

who ferrets wife
and life into a closet

when tornadoes form.
Praise heaven's realm,

the calm that overwhelms
our sullen Mississippi

of the mind, the quiet
wrenched from storm

now just the storm itself
turned to music absent

pain. Only rubbish
left behind and exhausted

trees relieving the dead
of the weight of the dead.

Praise the hole the wind
bores in the sky, warden

of the world's wonders.
Praise the love aimed like

a child with some glass
to immolate the ants.

Miracles are not so hot
on heat and pleasures

of the char. Leave that
to the light, the kind

that knows no kindness.
No clarity, we know,

is harvested from fields
of smoke. No mourning

either in the blood-red
trucks and water

they must summon. So much
depends upon them not

uncoiling their ropes,
serpents in the desert

of a suburb barbed
with rebar jutting

from its gut. Praise
to the clearing sky

and pastor's story.
Tell it again and again.

When he came to
and exited the closet,

the closet was closest
to a soul, the house its body

now gone, departed.
Dearly departed, the sole

of God's boot has left
its impression everywhere.

THE RESTAURANT

First, some small pulleys and levers,
artichoke hearts in a wire nest,

some sort of sauce made of beet
or the blood of innocents.

Like tiny explosions of joy in our mouths.
Then came a generous round

of toggles and red buttons. We clicked
and teased them with our tongues.

Hard to tell why the chef's fingers
arrived on a platter of Bibb

and not frisée, the vinaigrette so pungent.
Still, we licked our fingers clean,

could have made a meal of them,
if not for the pasta of piano-wire

consistency, which the waiter, a sallow fellow
from the East somewhere, unwound

from the coil of his neck. We pardoned him
his hoarseness, so long as he kept his distance

like we kept pets: well loved and chained
in closets, unfinished basements.

Someone took a tumble in the kitchen.
We heard the cloches roll,

the sobbing after. Managers apologized.
They begged us. They always do before the end,

which, they promised, would be lovely.
We simply wanted the check, but already

a few nervous men in white approached us
with the detonator, its plunger shimmering

in candlelight, the eyes of all the other guests
attendant on us, their hands raised for the clap.

HOW AM I DRIVING?

Am I observing all the signs
you offer of your fuel-efficient

anger? Are the giant wheels
of all my best intentions turning

in a way that makes you feel
so vital to their tread?

Are your kids home safe?
Do the dead still talk to us

from roadside floral wreaths?
Wherein lies the newly paved

highway to your happy life?
Let me take you there. Room

inside my leather cab will cost you
nothing but a friendly nod,

a call to dispatch to declare
that I was good, maybe even saved

a kitten from a phone pole
connecting all of us. I once filled

potholes with impatience. You ran
all over them. The pressure, I mean.

Do I deny the souped-up Vette
its blower? Must I spurn the Jetta

simply for its Nazi origins?
The Gestapo always knew how

everyone was driving. Does that
raw analogy affect you? Is it apt?

Do you read my blinkers as just
self-policing? How fared

the Yankees on their road trip?
Can they please grow facial hair?

My daughter is in eighth grade now.
Is it wrong to say I love her

but don't like her? Grade:
we talk about a road that way,

also meat and eggs. Grade me
on my shepherding. Tell me

I am doing well, better than
last week. I was drinking,

it was raining, you were crying,
and the dog deserved it.

DAISY CUTTER

Romancer of the mania of jungle,
disseminator, clear-cut jab in the gut
of a tiny island dense in foliage
and communists. Or just a tryst
between a bomber and a bunker,
and one of them will get its heart
so badly broken. News flash: both do
solemnly swear to leave the other
empty, just a shell at the root of all
our injury. Let us refer to this
instrument by its skin and not
its powder and potential. Finches,
crows: they cry when a red-tailed scours
the sky, even mob and ankle-bite
till it demobs. But what can one do
with a bomb like you, inscrutable
as stone and just as polished?
Bullet-shaped Sphinx to the Egypt
of our worst intentions, you descend
on a parachute's held breath,
then shiver the timbers of whatever
state is under harsh examination.
Metal Martin Luther nailing to the door
of the front page news a little hole
crowded by charred palms, our palms
are open to you, up until the moment
we rush them to our ears and brace.

THE FIELD, A SERIES OF LOW BUILDINGS, A DISTANT ROAD

What if the planet simply shrugged its green
delusions, whole canopies snapped at the root?
What if the waters that divide us rose up

to satellites gouging the night's blank slate?
What if the end were as colorless as real
estate, odorless as a box of hypodermics,

if Soviet-era bombs still carried the worst
we've dreamed: big blisters of incendiaries
or just the nerve to harbor nerve gas?

Because last night, a blogger in England
correctly showed the world some crumpled finger
of a missile pointed at the heart of rubble

near Damascus and, from that far,
became a god who hath wrought unto us
such holy surveillance, he of little faith,

little internet wraith. The nerve of him.
Sarin, Sarin: said that way, it sounds like pop.
But how are we to sing? And what if the night—

millions of backlit screens atop mahogany
in millions of split ranches, loft apartments
perched on the zenith of oblivious towns—

what if the night stopped listening, stopped
watching through the night, through the slick,
frictionless windows bought on clearance,

amortized and polished? Today, for instance,
some rebels have their heads removed
by chain saw, but this, we understand, is just

the planet spinning as it has, as it will,
ancient in its choreography. What is worse:
the fact or the fact it keeps occurring?

The house shattered to tinder or the factory
that spits munitions out like teeth? What are we
to sing among the wreckage? What the hell?

What the hammer? What the chain?
Even now, armies in fitful sleep rehearse
their grim *danse.* Even now, treetops shiver

black-pocked leaves on the blacktop
and frozen lawns at the borders of suburbia.
Even now, the bully barks, as he grinds

a little gravel in your face, *We're even now.*
But we're not. We're not even close.
From the safety of our mortgages and sugar

salve in early coffee, a morning unbloodied
as the rest, waters at lake's edge grow
eerily calm. Ducks disturb the viscous sheen

with dabbling, as do we, as we tune the TV
to a touch of death: some shooter and a grudge,
that roadside with cars tossed like a salad,

an airstrike and the shaky video to prove it.
As if we could look away. As if we could
power down and grab the running shoes,

shake the whole thing out of our heads.
As if the magnetism of the earth itself
did not pull us back to the couch. As if

we could design our days bereft of the field,
a series of low buildings, a distant road
that takes us to the happening,

which by now is just some scattered people
and a crater, a white dog with choke chain,
whose legs twitch uncontrollably.

As if we could design a less traumatic end.
As if we were designers, little animists
at the mount. There on the sunny balcony

of a rebel's apartment, the ashen chairs,
the makeshift grill (for even then they feed),
and such a tiny canister that carried the gas,

wrought from the land, stitched together
in a crumbling state, designed in Kosovo,
if design could ever govern in a thing so small.

OTHER BOOKS IN THE CRAB ORCHARD SERIES IN POETRY